CW01108519

Hessle
in old picture postcards

Patrick Howlett

European Library ZALTBOMMEL/THE NETHERLANDS

Bibliography:

Extracts from: Haltemprice Urban District Council Book issued to commemorate the Coronation of George VI in 1937.
Hessle: Its History, Curiosities & Antiquities.
Hessle Local History Society Publications.
All Saints' Church, A.S. Harvey.
The Story of Methodism in Hessle 1820-1977, H.F. Brown.
Stan Owen Archives.

Acknowledgements:

Miss Hilary Tyson for her invaluable assistance and support.
Miss Margaret Farrow for her help.
I should also like to thank the many residents of Hessle who have assisted me in so many ways with information, advice and the loan of photographs.

GB ISBN 90 288 6672 8
© 2001 European Library – Zaltbommel/The Netherlands

No part of this book may be reproduced in any form, by print, photoprint, microfilm or any other means, without written permission from the publisher.

European Library
post office box 49
NL – 5300 AA Zaltbommel/The Netherlands
telephone: 0031 418 513144
fax: 0031 418 515515
e-mail: publisher@eurobib.nl

Introduction

Hessle is a small township with a population of approximately 15,000 people, situated on the north bank of the River Humber. It lies to the west and adjacent to the City and County of Kingston upon Hull.

The first record of Hessle is in the Domesday Book, it was then named 'Hase' and in the record it is stated 'a Church is there and a Priest is there'. Hessle derives its name from 'Kiesel' which means 'a flint'. Hase was next spelt 'Hessell'.

The parish extended to the River Hull, embracing the present site of Kingston upon Hull, so that Hase or Hessle is much more ancient than Hull, which was once in Hessle. For nearly four centuries All Saints' Church at Hessle was the Mother Church to the Holy Trinity in Hull. In the early days, long before there was a place to bury the dead in Hull, the bodies of the deceased persons were carried to the parish church at Hessle for interment. It was a perilous journey, which was made by the river bank and many coffins, and attendants were swept away by the turbulent waves of the Humber.

Hessle has a great history. During the seige of Hull in 1642 the village suffered considerably for we find that the Parliamentarians pulled up the sluices and cut away the banks, thus flooding the surrounding neighbourhood and causing great destruction of property.

In the early years Hessle was little more than a large agricultural place with farms in the village, some close to the parish church and others on the outskirts. All the area of the village outside the centre, until the Enclosure Act of 1796, was open common land with no hedges or fences. This gave rise to the various 'Gates' as we know them, Eastgate, Northgate, Southgate and Swinegate.

According to the Domesday Survey there was 'an ancient ferry' operating between Hessle and Barton (which is on the south bank of the Humber). In 1315, following complaints of extortion on the ferry, King Edward I ordered that only the customary halfpence for pedestrians and one penny for horsemen was allowed to be charged. The ferry ceased to operate in 1882.

Although predominately an agricultural village, industry too played a part in the life and economy of the community. Since the 14th century until the 1960s chalk quarries were situated on the Hessle Foreshore which provided employment for a large workforce. The area had its own church, inn and several mill cottages were built for the employees. Shipbuilding became another important industry towards the end of the 17th century, which included building ships of war for the Government. During the First World War Livingstone and Cooper built shallow draught hospital ships for use in the Middle East. In the Second World War, Richard Dunston, still trading under the name of Henry Scarr, was responsible for building many types of vessels such as tugs and small coastal craft. Unfortunately, in 1994, after 97 years, Richard Dunston was the last of the Hessle shipyards to close.

At the first Census in 1801 Hessle had a population of 681 inhabitants and was a thriving and attractive community, which the merchants and bankers of Hull had begun to turn to in their search for a peaceful rural place to live. Several fine houses were built to be occupied by the wealthy people and many of the newcomers to Hessle became great benefactors to the village. The Hull, Selby and Leeds Branch of the North Eastern Railway opened on 1st July 1840. In November 1861 the village was lit by gas and by 1901 the population had risen to 3918.

In the early 1900s the tempo of life in the village was leisurely compared to life today, traffic was mainly horse drawn and slow. Everyone knew everyone else, news spread quickly and almost every aspect of life and death – physical and spiritual – could be catered for within the confines of the village.

Hessle's two most outstanding features span the centuries and offer a striking contrast between the medieval craftsmanship and modern technology. The earliest of these is the parish church that is of Saxon origin, but completely rebuilt in the reign of King Stephen and then between 1868 and 1870 it was restored and enlarged. The 15th-century perpendicular tower with octagonal spire rising to 170ft is a fine landmark. The latest and famous landmark is the Humber Bridge, which was officially opened by Her Majesty Queen Elizabeth II on 17th July 1981. Although the Humber narrows between Hessle and Barton, it is still more than one mile wide. The structural design therefore meant building the longest single span suspension bridge in the world (1410 m). This achievement was held until 1998 when Japan opened their Akashi-kaikyo Bridge (1991m).

Although there have been many changes over the years, Hessle is still a good place to live. In 1991 the population had risen to 13,818 and still new housing developments are taking place. It is pleasantly situated on the River Humber with many delightful walks, and…

As seen from the Western Hill,
the Village Church and Spire,
It is a very pleasant spot,
As any in the Shire.

Patrick Howlett

1   The people of Hessle gathering for a day of celebration to mark the Diamond Jubilee of Queen Victoria's reign in 1897. The picture shows the procession which formed at 1 p.m., opposite Mr. E. Saunder's public house, The Marquis of Granby, before proceeding to Hesslewood Hall, the home of Mr. H.J.R. Pease, who had offered the use of the grounds for the day. The procession, which was a mile long, was headed by the Wilberforce Band from Hull and followed by members of the Jubilee Committee. The children of the village, all decorated with medals, followed the official parties. Villagers followed the school children and Mr. Pease's large brake carried the aged population. The celebrations continued with 'a programme of sports, dancing, fairground rides and viewing the beautiful gardens and grounds of Hesslewood'.

Tea was served to the children and adults, after which there was dancing and music until dusk.

2   Here we see the funeral cortege of Constable Nettleton of the Hull Police Force. On 20th March 1905 in Prospect Street, Hull, he endeavoured to stop a runaway horse and cart and was knocked down and suffered fatal injuries. The funeral took place at Hessle. The Police Band met the cortege, which consisted of four coaches and two carriages at the Cottage Homes, whilst 200 policemen who had travelled to Hessle by train marched to meet the cortege at Hull Road. Thousands of people lined the route from Hull to Hessle and eventually the coffin with twelve policemen acting as pallbearers was carried into The Primitive Methodist Church, Southgate, for the Service. Afterwards interment took place in the Hessle cemetery in a grave adjoining that of Constable Nettleton's two brothers. He left a widow and four children.

3   Looking eastward down Tower Hill, the cottages on the right are still to be seen and are lived in. In the background can be seen the spire of the Wesleyan Methodist Chapel (now known as Tower Hill Methodist Church). The wall seen on the left has been demolished and another modern one erected, whilst many of the buildings on this side of the road have been replaced by modern flats built in a small cul-de-sac.

4 This early photograph shows the west end of the old Hull Road leading into the village centre with the Granby Public House in the background. This part of Hull Road was previously known as Cow Lane and was so named because the 'Cows' Gate' was sited at a point near the garage premises on the north side of the present Square. The buildings on the left were demolished in 1921/22 to create the open space now known as Hessle Square. These shops on the right of the picture are still trading – although in a more modern guise – and serving the people of Hessle.

5 Looking up Northgate as it appeared circa 1904. The children are gazing in the shop window of Mr. Charles Cowan, the village baker. The archway beyond the sunblind shows an effigy of a smiling man, this is dated 1851. The three cottages immediately following are some of the oldest in the village and in this year 2001 are still standing, but have been modernized. The last building we can see on the left is the United Methodist Chapel, which is now demolished. Opposite the baker's was a blacksmith's shop where the farrier Tommy Marriott shoed horses and mended cartwheels. Children would gather round and watch with fascination as the bellows brought the forge to white heat, horse shoes were beaten to size, shaped and applied to the hooves of patient shire horses and ponies. The blacksmith's was demolished in the early 1920s and a branch of the Co-op was built on the site.

6   Northgate in 1905 looking towards the parish church. The pond in the foreground was a favourite with children and cattle alike, but disappeared during the 1930s. At the corner of Trinity Grove is Brook Cottage, which is still standing and has been renovated in a pleasing way. This cottage is one of the oldest surviving farm buildings in Hessle. On the opposite side of the road was Mr. Mathison's farm, which was just one of three in Northgate. Next to the farm during this period was the Hessle Nursing Home, now a private residence.

North Gate, Hessle.

7   Here looking towards Tower Hill and Northgate corner we see what was commonly known as North Church Side and the entrance to Vicarage Lane on the right. The first shop seen here belonged to George W. Mallison who, at a later date, went into partnership with a Mr. Barlow to form Mallison & Barlow's Grocers and this was also the local post office. The building in the centre of this block has been many varied shops, but as we write it is now a public house. The buildings on the corner were demolished and a Co-operative Store opened here in 1925.

8 This photographer had a very attentive audience when he approached Eastgate in the early part of the 20th century. This area would be easily recognized today as apart from the farm seen in the background, which no longer exists, the houses and the gardens are exactly the same. The farm mentioned belonged to Edward Saunders, who besides being a farmer was also the licensee of the Marquis of Granby public house, situated on Southgate.

9   This half-timbered building at the top of Prestongate is one of the most photographed views of Hessle. The gentleman on the bicycle leaning on the lamp post is outside Myers Refreshment Rooms as these premises were in the early part of the 20th century. As we look down on the left, the group of people and carts we see are outside the George Inn, better known to the locals as 'Top House' and reputed to sell the best ale in Hessle! The white building next door was Wallis' shop and farm and they also carried on the business of local carriers. All the buildings in the foreground on the right were demolished and now a new retail shopping complex is situated here. The lady with the parasol and the gentleman in his boater look very elegant as they ascend the hill.

10   No one is quite sure where the name originates, but this is The Weir and there are stories of a small stream or weir on this site at one time. On the immediate left of the picture we see the tailor's shop owned by Mr. Darley. Next door was the Working Mens' Club and Institute; the shops we see sold various commodities, one being a newsagent. The houses were tenanted for many years but gradually have been converted to shops, making the whole of the west side commercial properties. We must remember all these premises seen here were only built in 1900.

11 This postcard dated 1911 shows the eastern side of The Weir. These houses look exceedingly elegant with the wrought iron railings and the ivy clinging to the exterior. Sadly, due to the Second World War, all the iron railings were taken to help with the war effort. Unfortunately, these family homes are now all commercial properties.

THE WEIR, HESSLE.

12 A 1920 view of Hessle, this photograph being taken from the church steps which overlooked the only open space in the village prior to the making of Hessle Square, when the buildings seen in the centre were demolished. To the right we see the Granby public house, which seems to feature in so many pictures of our village. The buildings on the left belonged to Bowser Appleton, clockmaker and fancy goods dealer, and there was also a sweet and tobacconists shop.

13 We have previously mentioned that Hessle was very agricultural and here we see trading taking place in an unusual commodity - GOATS! This is the only open space as seen in the preceding photograph, but in this view looking towards the church. The large house seen centre was at the time the home of one of the local doctors, but this was later demolished and the Church Hall was built on the site.

14 A 1906 view of South Lane looking towards The Weir. These elegant houses on the left were originally known as Eastbourne and Westbourne Villas. The houses have been well preserved as they still look as good in 2001. Sadly the balustrades seen on the top of the bay windows have all disappeared. The small building on the right on the end of the wall was the National Provincial Bank whilst the building on the other side of the entrance to Grove Hill became the Hessle Nursing Home, when they vacated the building on Northgate.

15 This postcard dated 11th October 1906 shows the main road from Hessle to Hull looking east. The building on the extreme right of the picture was once a laundry, next to it we see the entrance to Florence Avenue. The houses in the centre of the picture had various names such as Rose Villa, Woodbine Villa, Primrose Villa and so on. The horse and cart making its leisurely way to the centre of the village is passing the Hessle cricket field, the whole of one side of which, where the spectators sat, was beautifully shaded by large trees.

16 Swinegate looking east; the large tree overshadowing this picture stood in the Vicarage grounds and had to be felled as it became unsafe. The cottages seen beyond the tree are still in use. The light faced house in the centre of the picture has been, and still is, the home of the Coates family for many years. The wall on the right has disappeared and Hessle Library was built on this site in 1984; the other cottages seen are all still occupied.

17   All Saints' Church, Hessle, is essentially Early English in style with a perpendicular tower and an octagonal spire rising to 170 feet. This has, in days past, served as a landmark for the weary traveller and an aid to navigation for seafaring folk who sailed their craft, both large and small, upon the River Humber. In the latter half of the 19th century the church was restored and enlarged at a cost of £8000 increasing the seating capacity to 1000.

18 This view of the interior, looking eastward towards the nave, shows clearly the octagonal columns that were added during the church extension as mentioned in the previous picture. During this rebuilding the chancel was raised considerably, which displaced some of the memorials to well-known local personalities, which then were placed in other parts of the church. To the right of the picture can be seen the Lady Chapel and on the left St. Barnabas Chapel, where the organ is situated.

19 The Parish Hall (now known as the Town Hall) was built in 1897 and is situated on the northern end of South Lane near to the junction with Ferriby Road. The Hall was the headquarters for the Hessle Urban District Council prior to 1936. Since this date the fortune of this Hall has been varied having been taken over by Beverley Borough Council in 1973 on the formation of Humberside. We seem to have had a period of stagnation and then upon the reformation of the East Riding of Yorkshire it was sold back to the people of Hessle for the princely sum of £1. We now have a management committee who are responsible for the hiring of the hall and various rooms. The Hessle Town Council now has an office within these premises.

20 The Police Station, as it will be remembered by many of the older residents of Hessle, has seen many changes. The sign between the four windows on the front of the building shows that it belonged to 'The East Riding Constabulary'. Whilst still in use as a police station the main door was bricked up and a new entrance made to the right of the notice board at the end of the building. Also visible on the roof of the Town Hall, which is situated behind the station, can be seen the 'Air Raid Siren'. This caused many a sleepless night in the war years with its dreary tone heralding another air raid.

21 Looking from the east down Swinegate this view of All Saints' Church clearly shows the War Memorial in the form of a cross of remembrance for the dead of the First World War. The piece of wall seen on the left has long been demolished and a new library was built on this site in 1984.

Church Side, Hessle   PN1935

22 The river bank was a favourite spot for the local children, as behind the path and hedge was one of the local playing fields. This path ran eastward from Cliff Road to the boundary of Livingstone and Coopers Shipbuilding yard, where we see a ship tied up. At this point you had to walk round the shipyard which brought you out at the Haven where stood the Ferryboat Inn, which was a welcome sight for a tired traveller!

23   The new Wesleyan Methodist Chapel on Tower Hill. The Opening and Dedication ceremony on Good Friday 30th March 1877, was a joyous occasion for many people attending this historic event. Special trains were laid on to bring people from Hull to join in the celebrations and the chapel was packed. Despite only having seating for 600, 1000 people were present, up the aisles and pulpit steps, even the porches were crowded. Adjacent to the chapel is the schoolroom, which was built on the site of two old cottages and which was opened, again with great fervour, in 1911.

24 A well-known local beauty spot was, and still is, Little Switzerland. Where this name is derived from, who knows? As you descend this path into the wooded glade you behold the play place of many generations of Hessle children and, haste I to say, very popular with courting couples. It is known that there was one gas lamp at the foot of the steps, but it was very rarely seen working! Continuing on the path towards the river you came to a very low tunnel that went under the railway line, and when emerging into daylight you beheld the mill and St. Mary's Chapel.

25 The staff and children of Hesslewood Seamen's and General Orphanage in the early 1940s. The orphanage was founded in Hull and was situated on Spring Bank and as more room was required the orphanage moved to Hesslewood Hall, the former home of J.R. Pease Esq. JP in the early 1920s. The orphanage was founded for the benefit of needy children from any part of the country, but orphans of seafaring men had the first preference. The children attended local schools and were encouraged to take part in local activities as members of Scout and Guide troops etc. Notice the sailor uniforms worn by the boys, but in latter years these disappeared and all the children wore the same type of clothing as other children.

26 Looking west up Swanland Road towards the gates of Tranby Park we see the lodge at the entrance to Hessle Mount. This picturesque building must surely be one of the most photographed places in Hessle due to its situation and architectural prominence. The topiary of these trees and many others in the grounds were much admired by the passing public. This winter scene, bare trees and lack of tracks in the snow, possibly means this photograph was taken early in the day as this is one of the main roads to Swanland and was well used.

27 Hessle Haven as it appeared early in the 20th century. On the left of the picture we see the new slipway of Henry Scarr, shipbuilder, who had come to this site and opened his yard in 1897. Although a few private craft are still to be seen moored on this side of the Haven, the barge that is tied up on the west bank is probably bringing in coal from further inland. This was also the docking point for the Hessle to Barton Ferry at some time of its life. Dobson's shipyard seen here on the right did not have a long lease of life, merely lasting approximately five years.

The Haven, Hessle.

28 Tranby House was built early in the 19th century on land of approximately 12 acres, which was purchased from John Carlill by the Barkworth family. It was two-storeyed of white brick with stone dressings and included the usual stables, coach houses and a walled garden. Accounts for buildings and fitting out the house dated 1806 specified, amongst other things, mahogany doors. The family connection continued until the death of Algernon Henry Barkworth in 1945. The house and property were put up for sale and purchased by the Local Council for £6400. On 5th September 1945 Tranby House opened as the Upper School of Hessle County Secondary School (now Hessle High School). Many additional buildings have been built, but it is not difficult, when viewed from Heads Lane, to still see the fine old Georgian house of almost two hundred years ago.

29   Algernon Henry Barkworth JP was a bachelor and the last member of the Barkworth family to inherit Tranby House. He was one of the lucky survivors of the Titanic, which whilst on its maiden voyage hit an iceberg and sank on 15th April 1912. He probably owed his life to his fur coat that he wore over his lifebelt, this gave him extra buoyancy and warmth when tossed about in the icy sea, until he was able to climb into a lifeboat. He died on 7th January 1945.

30 This must be one of the first pictures of the new Hessle Square, which was created in 1921-22 to make it easier for traffic coming down Prestongate going on to Hull Road. Previously it had to take a sharp left into Southgate, passing the old Admiral Hawke Hotel, and within a short distance a sharp right turn into Hull Road passing all the buildings seen on the right here. The church spire is plainly seen towering above Mayes' fruit, vegetable, fish, game and poultry shop. The largest building was at this time a sale room at one side and a boarding house at the side where we see the arched doorway.

Village Square, Hessle.

31 You know it is cold when you see the water of Hessle Haven frozen and ice floes on the River Humber itself. This was the winter of 1947 and a very bad one it was. The war had only been ended for two years and rationing was still in place. One of the commodities rationed was coal, so people could not have big fires as a matter of course. You often saw people walking on the Humber bank looking for driftwood or indeed anything that would burn. It was not unknown for certain cheeky young lads to hurl abuse at the train drivers hoping that they would throw lumps of coal at them. These were swiftly gathered up and taken home to supplement the ration.

32 On 28th February 1928 a very well-known local publican died. Mr. George Cograve was the landlord of the Admiral Hawke for many years and, as seen here, a great many people turned out to pay their last respects on 1st March. No, the funeral was not the next day but two days later as this was a leap year! The name of Cograve was well-known in Hessle because, as we see the cortege is drawn up outside of the baker's shop, this also belonged to the family. The man leading the horse is Mr. Mayes, who was always the first customer of Mr. Cograve every lunch time as he opened for business. This picture also gives us a good view of 'Baker's Arch' with the smiling face of a previous owner of this property with the date 1851 under the effigy.

33 There are many local boys and girls on this picture who are still around and living in Hessle to this very day. The picture was taken outside of the Primitive Methodist Chapel, which was situated on South Lane, and judging by the children's clothes this would be the Sunday School Anniversary Concert. From the number of children present it would seem that Sunday School was very popular, but it should be noted that the girls even then outnumbered the boys! This is a wartime photograph taken 1942-1943.

34 Looking north along Barrow Lane, in this early picture it will be seen there is no modern development on the left and there is quite a gap beyond the white houses in the centre. Although it is not evident these houses are on the other side of Salisbury Street, which runs from Barrow Lane to The Weir. Houses filling these open spaces were built between the two world wars.

35 Today's traveller riding on a bus between Hessle and Hull along Hull Road would hardly recognize these premises, which stand at the corner of River View. This was a sub post office and grocery store owned by the Botham Bros, who previously had premises on Southgate and who are seen here standing in the doorway. The other gentleman with his hand on the van was Mr. Smith, another local shopkeeper. The products that you can see advertised in the window bring back many memories.

36 Brook Cottage standing on the corner of Trinity Grove and Beverley Road is one of the oldest premises in Hessle and was very near to the village pond. We presume this was the home of the farm foreman who was employed by one of the many farms in this area. You can see on this picture that there is a profusion of climbing ivy on the gable end and this was to prove troublesome in future years, the whole wall having to be demolished and rebuilt.

37 All the houses seen here on Ferriby Road are still occupied and no commercial development has taken place. In fact it looks very much the same if you were to view this today in 2001. The entrance to Gladstone Street is where we see the house with the chimneys, the lamp post on the right is standing on the corner of Chestnut Avenue.

38 Mr. Wrightson seen here leaning against his wagon was the local window cleaner who lived in Eastgate. You can clearly see the tools of his trade, his ladders protruding from the inside of the cab over the horse. The two men at the rear of the wagon, we assume, were two of his employees.

39 As you walk along the foreshore towards North Ferriby, having first passed the mill on the right, you come upon this scene. The cottage was the home of the foreman of the chalk and whiting works, which were nearby. We can see chalk being loaded on the barge at the end of the jetty. The aforementioned cottage has been virtually demolished and rebuilt, it is now known as the Country Park Hotel and is a very popular watering hole for weary travellers!

40 Here we capture the essence of wartime Britain, the never-ending queues for the various commodities that were essential to everyday life. This queue at Norman Johnson's fruit and vegetable shop, which was just on the right as you went up Prestongate from The Square, is for a far more luxurious item, which had not been seen for many years. In fact many of the younger children had never seen them at all and wondered what those strange curved yellow things were. Bananas, what are they, what do you do with them? As you look over the people in this queue towards the right of the picture you can just see the roof of one of the four air raid shelters that stood in The Square throughout the war years.

41 It looks a cold and frosty morning, judging by the frost on the roof of the Church Hall in this picture. This hall was built on the site of what had been a doctor's residence and later a hotel. These were demolished and the hall built in 1937, the foundation stone being laid by the Archbishop of York, Dr. William Temple. This shows the war years when, throughout this period, it was used as a First Aid Post and Ambulance Station and was manned constantly, some of the staff being seen on this photograph.

42   Looking to the needs of their steeds these Free French soldiers, who descended upon Hessle in 1944, are carrying out daily maintenance on their tanks. The building in the centre is easily identified as the Darley's Hotel, which is situated on the north side of Boothferry Road. On the right of the picture, shrouded in mist, is the shop that was known locally as the Northfield Co-op Shop. The whole of the north carriageway between the entrance to the Hessle County Secondary School and the Broadway garage roundabout was closed to traffic and given over to the parking of the tanks. The cat in the foreground seems oblivious to all that is going on around it.

43 This Christmas greeting which comes from Old Mill, Hessle Waterside, gives an excellent view of Hessle's unique five-sailed mill, which stood very near the Humber Foreshore. Between the mill and the chapel was the entrance path that led to Little Switzerland, a popular beauty spot, well known to many courting couples! At the foot of the mill we see St. Mary's Church, which was a Chapel of Ease for All Saints' Church.

44 In today's world this must be a very unusual sight, but very common to the residents of Hessle prior to the Second World War, as in Northgate there were at least three farms. The gable end that we see to the left was Mathison's farm and further down on the right beyond the white building was Teal's farm. These beasts will be going back to the open fields, which have unfortunately disappeared for ever, as there is no open space left until you get past Boothferry Road.

45 Walking into this shop, or just walking past it, you were immediately assailed by the smell of freshly-ground coffee. Standing as it did on the corner of Ferriby Road and The Weir, Field's was a very popular shop. Not only was it a grocer's, but as you entered the door and turned to the left you came to what was Hessle's main post office. Messrs. Mallison & Barlow had previously owned these premises.

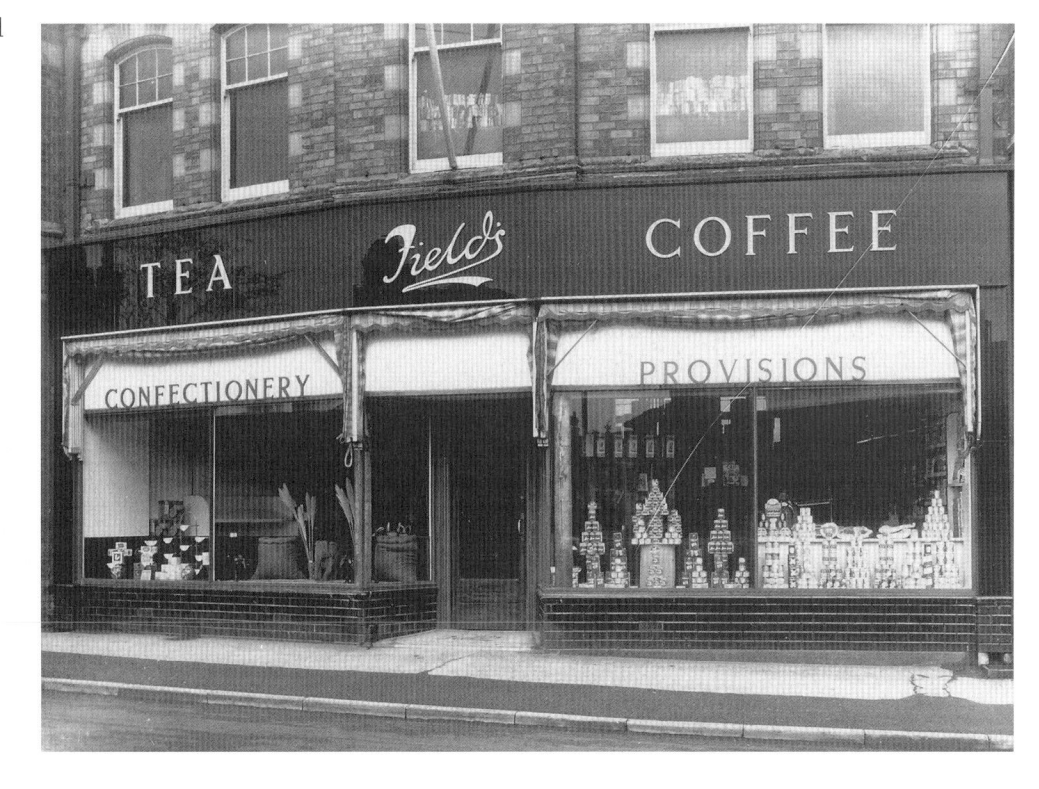

46 Admiring boats tied up in the Haven is Mrs. Doris Westoby, a well-known Hessle lady seen here leaning on the fence to the left of the picture. The Haven was well known to local boat owners and also as Henry Scarr's shipbuilding yard. These were famous for their side launches of ships into the Haven on a high tide, where many of the assembled youths watching this event received a good soaking as the water swamped their vantage point, which was on the wall opposite the yard.

47 Popularly known as Cemetery corner, this was the view in 1938. The date is quite accurate, as the picture showing the farm known as Swiss Cottage appeared on a 1939 calendar. The children we see walking up the road are possibly on their way home from the village school to the recent housing developments of Northolme, Sunningdale and Richmond Roads. I presume the car seen here is stationary, as it is being overtaken by a horse and cart!

48 Looking at the absence of cars and other vehicles it must surely be a new development, this picture being taken round about 1937-1938. It is unique due to the fact that all the houses on the Buttfield Road Estate are semi-detached. You can just see the entrances to Margaret Grove and Jill Grove on the left and the only other turn off on the right is Bon Accord Road, which is just past the bend. The name Buttfield is derived from the fact that on this site many years ago there were two archery butts, where the local yeomen were expected to practice their skills.

49 The centre piece of this aerial view is self-evident, All Saints' Church, but Hessle has the unique feature of having two churches with spires within a hundred yards of each other. In the foreground we can see the northern corner of The Square and the Granby public house. The year of this photograph must be circa 1925, as the new Hull Co-operative Shop on the corner of Northgate and Swinegate has yet to be built. Many of the buildings seen on this photograph, especially on Tower Hill, have been demolished.

AEROFILMS SERIES AIR VIEW OF HESSLE No. 12673 A

50 Many of the present residents may not know that Hessle once had two thriving shipyards, both on the east and west banks of the Haven. This view shows the yard of Livingstone & Cooper and as the stocks are full with lots of ships being built I can only surmise that this is dated around 1918, towards the end of the First World War. The large open field seen in the centre of the picture is now a housing development. To the right of this field can be seen one of Hessle's more unusual landmarks, Hall's Folly, this was situated within the grounds of Hessle Lodge, both of which were demolished when the Buttfield estate was built.

51 At the peak of its era this view shows Hessle railway station at its very best. In the left foreground we see the line going behind the west-bound platform leading to the goods yard. The bridge between the platforms was moved and extended when between 1904 and 1906 the two lines were replaced with four because of the increase in popularity of this form of travel. The large building seen here housed the booking office, station master's office and lamp room. The loading bay on the right was used for unloading horse-drawn carriages.

52 Situated on the south side of Swinegate this building is still extant, although not as we see it in this picture, having been considerably modernized. It was known as the School for Domestics and was funded by Henry Lock, a banker, who resided at Hessle Mount; his wife administered the school and appointed Lydia Levitt as the mistress. It was used from 1840 to 1870 and may have continued after this date. During this period the mistress Lydia Levitt married and became Mrs. Lydia Stather.

53 A very unusual sight for a place the size of Hessle, three fire engines in The Square all lined up for a photograph. On the extreme right of this picture we see Captain 'Gus' Newton, Hessle's Fire Chief, who when not in uniform was the proprietor of two newsagents' shops. In the centre, behind the second engine, you can see the fire station with one of its doors open and this is why this picture is unusual, Hessle only had one engine. I wonder where they had borrowed the others from, and why? I think this is just pre-war and was a show of strength for the benefit of the local populace.

54 An advertisement for the Hull Savings Bank, The Weir, Hessle, in 1926. Opening hours at this branch were limited, but as this was the year of the General Strike and unemployment was rife, little money was available for saving.

THE BEST BANK FOR SAVINGS IS
————————————THE SAVINGS BANK

HULL - -
SAVINGS
- - BANK

The WEIR
- - HESSLE

OPEN MONDAY   WEDNESDAY   SATURDAY
      6.30 to 8 p.m. 2 to 3.30 p.m. 6.30 to 8 p.m.

THE ONLY CERTIFIED TRUSTEE
     SAVINGS BANK IN THE DISTRICT

Hessle Depositors may transact any business at the Head Office during the hours the Hessle Branch is not open

Head Office :—GEORGE STREET, HULL

55   This is a view of Hessle in 1906 as seen from the top of Ferriby Road looking east towards Hull. Although not a steep hill it seemed to pull when going up, but in the winter it was very good for sledging because there was very little traffic. If you went to the same place today you will find it impossible to reproduce this view due to the fact that trees now obscure the houses seen on the right. On the left the building of a School and Residential Home means that Hessle's two spires can no longer be seen.

56 First Lane is on the eastern edge of the Hessle boundary with Hull, but this has not always been so. The very name of First Lane suggests that there must have been more and this is quite true as Anlaby Park Road was known as Second Lane and Pickering Road as Third Lane. All the above were part of Hessle until 1929, when the boundaries changed and Hessle lost the Second and Third Lane to Hull. The drain seen here has been modernized with a deep drainage scheme and is now completely enclosed and no longer seen. Apart from this, the view remains the same.

57 The year is 1912 and this montage of Hessle views shows a diversity of subjects ranging from the church interior to the path through Little Switzerland and the mill on the Foreshore.

58 In the 1930s the Gas Showroom at Hessle was in a commanding position on the corner of Southgate and The Square, which itself was fairly new. The stock in the window on the left shows the very latest in modern cookers whilst in the other window can be seen gas coppers and gas rings. Notice also the exterior lighting is all gas and very ornamental. Business must be slack if the two young ladies have time to pose for the photographer (incidentally, if anyone knows their identity please contact the author). Present-day residents will recognize these premises as belonging to Innes, photographers.

59 Hessle Square as it appeared in the early 1960s when, due to the influx of increased traffic on the roads, the centre of The Square was given over to the parking of cars and a bus terminus was established. As we noted previously many buildings were demolished to make The Square in 1921-1922 and we now seem to be filling in all the space created then. This has further changed and the car park seen here has now been landscaped and paved, which has reduced parking facilities considerably.

The Square, Hessle.

60 This well-known fruit, vegetable and flower retailers, Manley's of Hessle, situated on the corner of Northgate and Tower Hill, conducted business here for many years. This family had their own smallholding and orchard and obviously much of the produce sold was home-grown. These premises where known as The Exchange at the turn of the century, later becoming a draper's establishment. The building has a long history, the deeds going back to 1743, which was two years before Bonnie Prince Charlie returned to claim the English throne.

61 This imposing cinema was built in 1936-1937 to replace the 'Star Cinema', which burnt down in 1936 and was situated on Hull Road between Victoria Street and Edward Street. The 'Plaza' was situated at the eastern end of The Square, being more central, and was a much-loved place of entertainment for all the residents of Hessle with prices to suit all. The first film to be shown on the day it opened was 'Rose Marie', starring Jeanette McDonald and Nelson Eddy. The programme changed every three days running from Monday to Wednesday and Thursday to Saturday. There were no showings on Sundays in those days, as the Sunday opening was a wartime innovation.

62   Many changes had taken place to all the houses seen on the right of this picture, from being a row of desirable residences to a row of shops. These changes took place over many years, but I believe the first change was when Mr. Smallwood moved his butcher's shop from round the corner in Prestongate into number 2 The Weir. Other traders followed suit and we soon had a diversity of goods on offer, ranging from Holtby's Farm shop, Sokells the Stationers, Taylor's Furniture Store and a chemist shop. Looking at this picture closely I do believe that there are two houses left, but I do not think they lasted much longer as private dwellings after 1957.

63 'Little Switz', as the people of Hessle affectionately know this local beauty spot, was created centuries ago. The quarrying of chalk moving ever into the chalk face came to a standstill on the eastern side of the excavations, due to the fact that the chalk had disappeared and gravel was now being quarried. Under the circumstances this site was abandoned and further quarrying pushed northwards into the countryside. Notice the single lamp stand, minus the lamp referred to previously. The steps and path made a convenient short cut into the village for the people who lived and worked here on the foreshore.

64 As the name suggests Station Road led from very near the village centre to the local railway station. It starts at the southern end of Southgate and terminates at the station. The place at which this photograph was taken is no longer a road bridge but now, sadly, just a footbridge spanning the tracks. The road on which the car is standing bears off to the left leading directly into Southfield, where some of Hessle's older houses stand. The houses on the left are between 1918 and 1939 developments, but the larger houses seen in the distance were built circa 1900. On the right the open fields, known locally as 'Wallis's Fields', became another housing development in the early 1950s.

65 This is one of the platoons of the Hessle Home Guard formed in 1940 to help defend Britain when there was a threat of imminent invasion by Germany. They mainly consisted of enthusiastic younger men, who had not yet been called up, and many veterans of the First World War. This photograph was taken possibly in 1943-1944 and the houses in the background have not changed in appearance, except for the lowering of the tall chimney stacks. As the war progressed in favour of the Allied Forces the Home Guard was disbanded in November 1944.

66 Hessle's victorious school choir assembled here with their trophies. This would be the first of many photographs taken on the new school playing fields of the Hessle County Secondary School, which was opened in 1927. Mr. Herbert Calvert was appointed to the post of headmaster and the school choir was his pride and joy, winning many prestigious awards over the years. In 1946 the choir was invited to perform on the radio and did so giving a half-hour recital on the BBC Home Service one Sunday evening.

67 Your carriage awaits, Sir! Outside the church we see the carriages of the local gentry waiting for their owners to leave the Service and be transported to their country houses, mainly situated to the west of the village. This would be a regular Sunday sight for the local residents.

68 In this picture of Hessle Haven, it is apparent many changes have taken place. The shipyard is still very busy producing many varied types of vessels such as tugs and trawlers. In 1966 the firm of Richard Dunston built the sail training vessel Sir Winston Churchill, which has only recently gone out of service. The small private craft seen moored on the western bank afforded many hours of enjoyment to their owners, not so much sailing as messing about with them. The strip of land in the right background had been the site of three shipyards at various times.

HESS.22F   THE HAVEN, HESSLE

69 Looking west from Station Road bridge towards Woodfield Lane bridge we see the modern improvements that were made when the line was upgraded to four tracks, between 1904 and 1906. The station took on a whole new appearance and many improvements for passengers' comfort were made. To the left can just be seen the signal box, behind which was the water softening plant. To the rear of this platform were the goods yard and coal handling plant. The opposite platform, which served passengers travelling to Hull, was well covered and incorporated some of the early buildings from the 1840s, which are seen here under the platform roof. This station had an enviable reputation for turnout and cleanliness in the pre-war years.

HESSLE STATION, LOOKING WEST

70 Swinegate looking west towards the church. The trees on the left where in the grounds of what was known as the School for Domestics and past there the cottages are still to be seen. The farmer seen here is possibly Mr. 'Rapper' King, leading the cart of hay into the farm that stood at the rear of Holly Lodge. This was a large house, which stood where these gardens are seen; sadly this was demolished in the 1960s.

71 Southfield, one of the first new developments after the railway came to Hessle due to it being situated virtually on the doorstep of the station. This meant that many businessmen were able to move out of the city of Hull and commute to their offices with ease. The roads at this time had no kerb stones, simply a row of trees to differentiate between the footpath and road. All the houses are quite large and would doubtless employ lots of domestic help.

72 These houses were built in Davenport Avenue in the late 19th century for the more well-to-do residents of Hessle, who would no doubt have business connections elsewhere. It would seem that the west side of the city of Hull was a popular place to reside. As we all know the prevailing wind in England is from the south-west and therefore would not bring the odious smell of the fish docks wafting this way. All these houses seen here still exist, but many have been turned into flats due to the cost of the upkeep of such large premises.

73 This well-known corner of Hessle has seen many changes, but as we write, these premises are being completely renovated in this year of 2001. The advertisement is taken from a 1926 Hessle Year Book. All these properties were only built in 1900 and despite many alterations the upper storeys have seen no changes. The advertisement speaks for itself in telling people where the post office is situated and the type of goods they are offering for sale.

Mallison & Barlow
LIMITED.

HIGH CLASS GROCERS
AND
PROVISION MERCHANTS

Post Office Buildings
Hessle

Telephone: 31 HESSLE

74   The building seen here will bring back memories of childhood to many 'older' Hessle residents, situated as it is in The Hourne. This was the first building erected of the National School and consisted of three classrooms. It was opened in 1856 for the children of Hessle and was greatly influenced by the Church of England. The school was much enlarged with a girls' department adjoining this building, which then became the infants' department. A boys' school was built in 1912 on the other side of the two cottages seen on the right. The name of Miss Lickiss must surely come to mind when you see this photograph, if you are one of the 'older' people!

75 Although, strictly speaking, this is not a picture of Hessle, it will evoke many memories to a lot of Hessle residents. The Blackburn Beverley aircraft seen here was manufactured at Brough, which is only a few miles west of Hessle and a great number of the workforce were Hessle men. This photograph shows the apron in front of the flying school, which is situated down Skillings Lane. The factory now belongs to British Aerospace and is still employing many Hessle people.

76 A familiar view to many people as you walk along Tower Hill towards The Weir. This scene has little changed, the only modern properties are seen on the left of the picture and are known as Tower Hill Mews. Looking across the Memorial Park we see Hessle's twin spires – All Saints' Church and Tower Hill Methodist Church. Both of these places of worship are still well used by the people of Hessle, not only as places of worship, but for many community activities.